# Arts and Crafts
## GARDENS

# Arts and Crafts
# GARDENS

WENDY HITCHMOUGH

V&A Publications

First published by V&A Publications, 2005
V&A Publications
160 Brompton Road
London SW3 1HW

Distributed in North America by Harry N. Abrams, Inc.,
New York

ISBN 1 85177 4483

Library of Congress Control Number 2004111387

A catalogue record for this book is available from the
British Library.

Designed by Broadbase

**Half-title page:** M.H. Baillie Scott, stained glass window,
Blackwell, 1898. © Martin Charles

**Front jacket illustration:** Ernest Gimson, Rodmarton
Manor. See p.49.

**Back jacket illustration:** Robert Lorimer, Earlshall. See p.36.

**Frontispiece:** Edwin Lutyens, Les Bois des Moutiers.
Photograph by Andrew Lawson.

**Right:** William Robinson's garden, Gravetye Manor. See p.14.

Printed in China

V&A Publications
160 Brompton Road
London SW3 1HW
www.vam.ac.uk

# CONTENTS

6  ORIGINS OF MODERN GARDENING

20  BACK TO NATURE

32  DEFINING THE STYLE

58  A SENSE OF PLACE

82  LIVING IN A GARDEN


93  FURTHER READING

94  GARDENS TO VISIT

95  INDEX

# ORIGINS OF MODERN GARDENING

The creation of the Arts and Crafts style of gardening involved a gentle revolution in lifestyle and design. Whereas the Victorian gardens that preceded them were designed with an element of formality, to be surveyed from a distance, the relationship between Arts and Crafts houses and their gardens was open and dynamic. Finely crafted paths and pergolas carried the architectural lines of the house into its garden setting, and semi-glazed doors, generous verandas and terraces diminished the boundaries between the living spaces of the house and the garden beyond. Victorian pastimes, which had revolved around the rituals of the drawing room, were abandoned for the great outdoors, and Arts and Crafts artists and designers laid claim to the garden as their inspiration and their canvas.

The Arts and Crafts garden was defined by a progressive, almost wild approach to planting restrained within a clear, architectural structure. The design of the garden was integrated with the design of the house as architects strove to root their buildings into the landscape – to diminish the hard-edged, man-made imposition of architecture by developing a new reverence for nature and her materials. An Arts and Crafts conceit that the architect should specify every detail of the house, from the

latch on the garden gate to the napkins on the dinner table, led to the invention of the garden as a sequence of outdoor rooms. This coincided with a determination among Arts and Crafts clients to sidestep the strict codes of conduct associated with the Victorian drawing and dining rooms and enjoy a less conventional lifestyle by making the most of their gardens.

Thousands of annuals were produced in greenhouses to create the brightly coloured geometric patterns in Victorian gardens; these plants were relegated to the compost heap the moment that they were past their prime. In Arts and Crafts gardens, however, the planting was designed to reflect the changing seasons, and as a result the balance shifted between architecture and nature. The celebration of the voluptuous abundance of nature rejected the rigid control of Victorian bedding schemes. Sunflowers, hollyhocks, old-fashioned roses and pinks found favour in planting schemes that were romantic and provocative. Stone paths narrowed between cascades of lavender and catmint. Pergolas dripped with white wisteria and perennials were allowed to fade and bow and run to seed.

At its most ambitious, the Arts and Crafts border was elevated to an art form. Painters such as Alfred Parsons and George Elgood owed their commercial success to a vogue for idealized images of hazy summer borders. Gertrude Jekyll captured her perennial effects

OPPOSITE
Frank Lloyd Wright,
Meyer May House, Grand
Rapids, Michigan, 1908.
© Balthazar Korab Photography

ABOVE
Thackeray Turner,
Westbrook, 1899–1900.
© Martin Charles

in hand-coloured photographs. These images were lavishly published in books and magazines, and made garden making seem easy and desirable.

Where Victorian gardening was a trade, relegated to hired hands, Arts and Crafts gardening revolved around a determination for the whole household to live and work in harmony with nature. As an outdoor room and an extension of the living spaces of the house, the Arts and Crafts garden fell within the feminine domain. Particularly for women, gardening became a fashionable hobby that was assertively modern and mildly controversial. It justified a literal loosening of Victorian stays and an allegiance to a topical, scientific trend for fresh air and exercise. It satisfied a profound and sensual desire to engage with nature while nurturing a more material celebration of home making.

No plot was too small for an Arts and Crafts approach to planning and planting. Town gardens were generally more succinct than their counterparts in the country. There was seldom the space or a requirement for a kitchen garden large enough to feed the household, or for bowling greens and tennis courts. However, while country gardens established a setting between the Arts and Crafts home and its natural landscape, town gardens were no less important in defining a communal setting, integrating nature into the townscape. The detailing of gates, steps and

pathways in suburban front gardens combined with unsophisticated cottage-style planting, set the tone for the neighbourhood as well as the individual home.

Gardening celebrities made the challenges of sowing and planting sound easy. William Robinson amassed a fortune as one of the first writers and publishers to recognize the potential of amateur gardening as a lucrative niche market. He began his writing career as horticultural correspondent for *The Times* before launching his own magazine, *The Garden*, in 1871 for amateurs and professionals alike. His magazines were filled with practical gardening tips aimed at the amateur. He offered advice on 'keeping cats out of Town Gardens', 'the habits of aphids and their relationship with ants' and 'when to weed'.

Robinson's lively and accessible style made *The Garden* a best-seller, but his influence in encouraging amateur gardening was more than equalled by his importance as an advocate for a new 'natural' style of planting. *The Wild Garden*, published in 1870, was the horticultural equivalent to treatises on architecture and design by John Ruskin and William Morris. Robinson's insistence that nature should provide the inspiration for garden design – that plants should be chosen to suit the conditions of site and soil and encouraged to grow as they might flourish in the wild – laid the foundations for modern gardening.

PAGE 11
**Edwin Lutyens and Gertrude Jekyll, Folly Farm, 1906.**
© Martin Charles

OPPOSITE
**William Robinson's garden, Gravetye Manor.**
© Martin Charles

BELOW
**Edward Lutyens and Gertrude Jekyll, Munstead Wood, north courtyard, designed from 1893.**
Richard Bryant/arcaid.co.uk

William Robinson,
Gravetye Manor.
© Martin Charles

For Victorians accustomed to cataloguing and controlling nature Robinson's ideas were either a heresy or a revelation, but they caught on. The simplicity and common sense of his philosophy was equally applicable to country estates and to small suburban plots. His revival of easy growing, native perennials such as Michaelmas daisies encouraged the amateur, and his tolerance for self-sown annuals, whether they appeared in borders or in cracks between the paving, favoured the lazy gardener.

Robinson called flowers by their common names. He encouraged his readers to experiment with natural effects: to plant annuals and perennials in irregular drifts; to grow wild roses through trees and shrubs and to rediscover their native meadow and hedgerow plants. His irascible nature and uncompromising, no-nonsense perspective made him suspicious of architects of the day who ventured to write about garden design. He dismissed their books and articles as 'art drivel', and was ill-disposed towards the partnerships between horticulture and architecture that were to define the Arts and Crafts garden. Nevertheless, his wild gardening laid the groundwork for an Arts and Crafts style of planting and his association with Gertrude Jekyll, who edited *The Garden* from 1900, effectively threw that planting style open to more adventurous creative collaborations.

Great Tangley, pergola. Plate
from *Some English Gardens*, after
drawings by George S. Elgood
with notes by Gertrude Jekyll,
1904.

Jekyll trained as an artist. She was an expert craftswoman and her social circle included innovators of the day such as John Ruskin, William Morris, Edward Burne-Jones and Dante Gabriel Rossetti. She was equally at home with the 'armourial classes' (those who could claim a coat of arms as their birthright). Her family background and social position made her a natural broker for country house and garden commissions. She was emphatically practical, with an insatiable curiosity into the technicalities of craftsmanship. Like William Morris, she was always game to have a go. Like Morris, too, her enthusiasm was contagious.

Jekyll was an outstanding communicator. From the 1890s, when she was obliged to abandon the finer crafts such as silversmithing and embroidery due to failing eyesight, she combined her creative and practical talents for gardening and garden design with garden writing and photography. Her articles for *The Garden* and her books, which were often illustrated with her own photographs, seduced her readers unwittingly into the values of Arts and Crafts.

Jekyll's own house, Munstead Wood in Surrey, framed an Arts and Crafts garden of iconic significance. The making of it was described in her first book, *Home and Garden*, as if it were the most ordinary thing in the world. She acknowledged the importance of employing an architect with a thorough knowledge of local building methods and

Edwin Lutyens, Munstead Wood, side door.
© Martin Charles

materials 'so that what he builds seems to grow naturally out of the ground'. She popularized the polemics of Arts and Crafts in her description of the oak timbers for the joinery as the 'same old friends' that she had seen growing as 'great grey trees' in the Surrey lanes. No trade was too menial for her pen, and her accounts of carpentry and bricklaying are compelling and idiosyncratic in their assumption that genteel readers might take these matters to heart.

The practicalities of gardening at Munstead Wood were eloquently set out in a succession of books and articles that inspired a generation of 'artist-gardeners' and made the house and its owner famous. Jekyll was inundated with letters and impromptu visitors. She despaired of the 'pertinacity of Americans and Germans and of journalists', and complained to Alice Morse Earle that 'if one has written a book one becomes in a way the public property of all idle and curious people'. Jekyll also became public property, however, for many serious amateur and professional gardeners and garden writers. Edith Wharton, Vita Sackville-West, Francis King and Beatrice Farrand all made pilgrimages to Munstead Wood. Her writing unwittingly directed the expeditions of a growing number of garden tourists who ventured out by train and bicycle to visit private gardens, uninvited, just as gardeners today seek inspiration from National Trust properties.

Edwin Lutyens, Munstead Wood, gate to spring garden.
© Martin Charles

The technological advances that made beautifully produced and illustrated books and magazines affordable to a growing number of middle-class homeowners opened even the most private and remote Arts and Crafts houses and gardens to public scrutiny. Magazines such as *The Studio*, *Country Life*, *House Beautiful* and *The Craftsman* provided their readers with plans, photographs and perspective drawings of houses and gardens, something that Victorian designers a generation earlier would have declined to do

out of deference for the privacy of their clients. They were published as a provocation.

Arts and Crafts houses and gardens may seem quaint and old-fashioned today. Their hallmarks of cottage-style planting, fine materials and traditional craft methods may seem reactionary, but at the turn of the century they were at the vanguard of modernism. Their 'cottage-style' simplicity was political. Their craftsmanship renounced industrialization and their practical, hands-on approach to gardening challenged the rigorous class and gender distinctions of Victorian polite society.

The books and magazines that created design celebrities and promoted the philosophy of Arts and Crafts across national, cultural and economic boundaries still convey the romance and idealism of the Arts and Crafts garden. They suggest an ease and affluence that masks modernity. Even when they were first published, the paintings and hand-coloured photographs of borders crammed with lupins, delphiniums and unruly roses were never overtly confrontational. However, they represented a seductive alternative to everything that was artificial and strait-laced in Victorian design, and thus effectively subverted the prevailing values of the day.

OPPOSITE
**Aubrey Beardsley, design for the cover of *The Studio*, 1895.**
V&A: E.451–1965

ABOVE
**James MacLaren, cottages at Fortingall, 1889.**
© Martin Charles

# BACK TO NATURE

At its most austere, the Arts and Crafts movement provided a recipe for life. It was healthy, wholesome and morally pure, and it suggested a resolution to the spiritual uncertainties and political inequalities that plagued Victorian consciences. For the less committed, however, it was a fashionable stance rather than a creed. A garden designed as an arena for reverence and enlightenment could be lifted from the pages of a magazine and scaled down to a suburban fashion statement. But the versatility of Arts and Crafts, and its relevance as a philosophy or as a style for the most committed clients of architect-designed country houses, for self-builders with a plot in Bungalow Heaven, and for those who could buy or rent in the fashionable garden suburbs, were in themselves political.

Arts and Crafts coincided with one of the biggest domestic building booms in history. It was perhaps the first pioneering design movement to appeal self-consciously to every level of society. The line of influence between supply and demand worked in both directions as modern, middle-class homeowners became more prevalent and more assertive in their spending habits. Clients and consumers were encouraged to engage directly in the creative processes of home making, and to accept a moral responsibility for design and manufacture.

In his influential text 'The Nature of Gothic', John Ruskin commanded his readers to look around their homes and recognize in their machine-made mouldings and perfect polishes the signs of slavery. Ruskin mixed politics with religion. He warned that the souls of men were destroyed by industrialization and that social insurgencies, 'the vain, incoherent destructive struggling for a freedom' among the masses, were directly related to the division of labour. He pleaded for 'a right understanding, on the part of all classes, of what kinds of labour are good for men, raising them, and making them happy', and he challenged his readers to use their purchasing power to demand 'the products and results of healthy and ennobling labour'.

Ruskin articulated a profound unease among the middle classes that the industrial sources of their prosperity were inextricably bound to urbanization and the degradation of manual labourers into 'fuel to feed the factory smoke'. Working men and women were encouraged to find salvation in the crafts as designers such as William Morris, Walter Crane and C.R. Ashbee made it their mission to improve the lives of the urban poor through lectures, workshops and classes. Amateurs were encouraged and improved under the auspices of the Home Arts and Industries Association, and magazines such as *The Craftsman* and *The*

*Home* offered templates and practical instructions, making the ennobling benefits of craft workmanship available to all.

Arts and Crafts became a vehicle for the dawning socialist, suffrage and nationalist movements of the late nineteenth and early twentieth centuries. Design reforms reflected the changing social and political values of the age, and pioneers such as William Morris used their influence as designers to further their political causes. Socialism was considered extreme enough to warrant ostracism in the nineteenth century, so that the political connections are difficult to pin down. They are implied rather than stated in Arts and Crafts publications. Morris was less restrained, however, in his lectures. His biographer J.M. Mackail quoted his account of a lecture on textile dyeing in 1889: 'the working men were good and attentive … and took our socialism well, in fact seemed to relish it'.

If 'The Nature of Gothic' instigated a broad connection between design and socialism, it also sowed the seeds for architecture as a statement of national identity. Ruskin described the physical distinctions of northern and southern landscapes seen through the eyes of a bird migrating over the surface of the world. He described the 'wolfish life', the moss and moorland of the north, as the core character for its architecture. He eulogized the 'mountain brotherhood

Edwin Lutyens, Les Bois des
Moutiers, Varengeville, Dieppe,
1898. Garden detail, arched
opening.
Andrew Lawson

ABOVE
Robert Anning Bell, 'Summer',
gesso panel, Les Bois des
Moutiers.
Wendy Hitchmough

OPPOSITE
Edwin Lutyens, Les Bois des
Moutiers. View through garden
to front elevation.
Andrew Lawson

between the cathedral and the Alp; this magnificence of sturdy power, put forth only the more energetically because the fine finger-touch was chilled away by the frosty wind'. As international exhibitions called for the design of pavilions to represent the culture and characteristics of each nation, and magazines such as *The Studio* created an international context for national identity, Ruskin's call for an architecture forged from the landscape and its climate inspired design movements embedded in the philosophy of Arts and Crafts. The Finnish National Romantic style, the American Prairie Style of Frank Lloyd Wright and the Amsterdam School were all responses to Ruskin's appeal.

Nature represented a primordial power as well as the bedrock of national identity for Arts and Crafts gardeners and designers. Scientific and rational challenges to the teaching of the Christian Church, as expressed in texts such as Charles Darwin's *The Origin of Species*, had shaken the foundations of Victorian society in the mid-nineteenth century. They gave rise to a host of doubts and alternative belief systems, including Spiritualism and Theosophy, which sought to reconcile modern, scientific knowledge with the religious needs of a culture raised on the prescriptive certainties of Church teaching and the prospect of salvation or damnation. Darwin's legacy at the turn of the century was a renewed interest in the ancient mysteries of nature and its elemental power.

BELOW
C.F.A. Voysey, design
showing birds and vine.
© Martin Charles

OPPOSITE
C.F.A. Voysey, The Orchard,
entrance porch, 1899.
© Martin Charles

The moon, the sea and the seven levels of spiritual elevation from the physical body to the astral plane appear to have shaped the design of one of Arts and Crafts' most extraordinary gardens, belonging to the Theosophist Guillaume Mallet, who was the client for Les Bois des Moutiers near Dieppe, designed by Edwin Lutyens. Nature assumed a spiritual potency, however, even in the most conventional Arts and Crafts houses and gardens. C.F.A. Voysey advised his fellow architects to make 'a more reverent study of nature and nature's ways ... The more we look in to nature, the more we feel the spiritual forces behind us all. It is this perpetual attention to the spirit in its purest manifestation that will improve our work, and so increase our happiness and usefulness.'

Voysey was typical of Arts and Crafts designers not only in his reverence for nature but also in his assertion that good design was a vehicle for the God-given thoughts and feelings of the architect. The house as a work of art, perfectly harmonious in its relationship with nature and balanced in every detail, was designed to have an improving effect upon the spirit as well as the lifestyle of the client. The birds and berries that decorate Voysey's designs are symbols of spiritual regeneration, and his signature heart motif signifies a profound, spiritual love rather than a valentine.

2.                                    3.

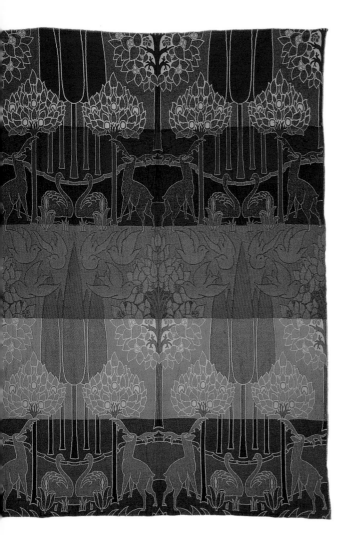

C.F.A. Voysey, hanging, woven
wool, for Alexander Morton
and Co., 1899.
V&A: T.150–1977

Painters and sculptors of the Arts and
Crafts movement were well versed in the
language of symbolism. Their clients thought
nothing of sending an unspoken message
encoded in a bouquet of flowers. By breaking
the traditional boundaries between arts and
crafts – between painting, design and the
decorative arts, and between architecture,
sculpture and the crafts – the Arts and Crafts
movement encouraged collaborations
and experiments. Designers adapted the
prerogative of painters to transport the
emotions and rouse the intellects of their
clients, while artists abandoned the
limitations of the canvas and created
complete interiors for their patrons.

The Arts and Crafts movement produced
some of the most exotic and extravagant
houses and gardens ever built, and the
fusion of art and nature that underpinned its
most ambitious designs, and its social and
spiritual ideals, permeated down through
every level of domestic design. Tree-lined
avenues with houses set back from the
pavements, framed within their own front
gardens, proliferated. As improvements in
public transport reduced the need for

Ernest Gimson, Alfred Powell,
cupboard painted with
Cotswold scenes, 1913.
Private collection

densely populated urban areas and home ownership became increasingly accessible to working couples and young families, the ideal of living in harmony with nature became commutable. Garden cities and garden suburbs were planned on the premise that even the most basic housing should incorporate sunlight, a garden and a view. Raymond Unwin, one of the pioneers of the garden city movement, regarded this slice of nature as a political wedge. Writing for the Fabians in 1902 he denounced the impoverished rows of many British urban terraces and their dingy back yards:

Hundreds of thousands of working women spend the bulk of their lives with nothing better to look on than the ghastly prospect offered by these back yards, the squalid ugliness of which is unrelieved by a scrap of fresh green to speak of spring, or a fading leaf to tell of autumn.

The regenerative potential of nature and beauty was central to architect-designed gardens for unique country houses; it was allowed to take shape as a consequence of market forces in fashionable suburbs and built into new communities with a socialist agenda. Garden cities were rooted in nineteenth-century philanthropy. Experimental model towns designed to accommodate factory workers, such as Bourneville near Birmingham in England, and Pullman, south of Chicago in the United States, were adapted to create a sustainable urban equivalent to life in a traditional village.

OPPOSITE
**Cavendish Pearson, houses in the Brentham Estate, Ealing, London.**
© Martin Charles

BELOW
**Tree-lined avenue, Bungalow Heaven, California.**
Wendy Hitchmough

# DEFINING THE STYLE

The Arts and Crafts garden was whimsical and romantic. It invited exploration. In larger gardens the plan was divided into a sequence of outdoor rooms, sometimes with hidden secret gardens and inner sanctuaries that flowered with spectacular intensity for a single moment in the gardening calendar.

Planting with year-round interest was seldom a consideration in the country. Although the flowering season was prolonged from early spring bulbs to autumn colour in town gardens, many of the larger Arts and Crafts gardens belonged to second homes, summer places and weekend retreats that were barely visited out of season. They were large enough to include outdoor rooms for croquet and tennis, terraces for afternoon tea and summer houses for secluded conversations. In gardens such as these a white garden filled with roses and phlox, for example, could simply be overlooked for eleven months of the year when it was not at its best. The garden had a poetic significance. It was the setting for memories of long, idle days in the sunshine. It was synonymous with summer and it retained a presence in the imagination long after its flowering season was finished.

Arts and Crafts designers drew on local craft skills and building traditions to honour a spirit of place in their work and to secure a continuity between 'old work' of a

OPPOSITE
**Robert Lormier, Earlshall, 1892.**
© Martin Charles

BELOW
**Robert Lorimer, plan of the garden at Earlshall.**
NAL: 108.A.9

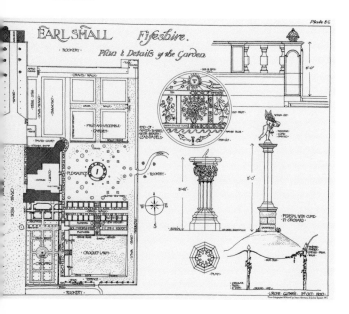

ABOVE
**Philip Webb, superfrontal, linen embroidered with silk and gold threads by May Morris, c.1896–7.**
V&A: T.379–1970

OPPOSITE
**Lawrence Johnston, Hidcote Manor, white garden, 1907.**
National Trust Photographic Library / Andrew Butler

pre-industrial age and their own vision of the simple life. Furniture designers adapted the solid simplicity and indigenous materials and styles of cottage and mission furniture, such as solid oak tables and rush-seated chairs passed down through generations. Textile designers and embroiderers studied the native flowers and artless delicacy of medieval textiles. Architects made the cottage a model for smaller town and country houses, but it required more than a little imagination to match traditional sources to the making of an Arts and Crafts garden.

Edith Wharton found 'the old garden craft' that modern Americans were seeking in Italian Renaissance gardens. She claimed that 'the old Italian garden was meant to be lived in … the grounds were as carefully and conveniently planned as the house', and recommended that her readers *think away* 'the flowers, the sunlight, the rich tinting of time' to find a deeper harmony in the fundamental plan:

The inherent beauty of the garden lies in the grouping of its parts – in the converging lines of its long ilex-walks, the alternation of sunny open spaces with cool woodland shade, the proportion between terrace and bowling green, or between the height of a wall and the width of a path. None of these details was negligible to the landscape-architect of the Renaissance.

The Ruskinian ideal that design should be honed by the climate and characteristics of a place and its people could be fudged in favour of a more classical approach, and British as well as American designers were inclined to blend their savage, Gothic designs with formal classical structures whenever it suited the occasion.

Nevertheless, the British Arts and Crafts movement was inseparable from a pioneering determination to preserve the nation's historic buildings. William Morris and Philip Webb were co-founders of the Society for the Protection of Ancient Buildings in 1877 and their passion for vernacular traditions inspired younger members of the society, including Sidney and Ernest Barnsley, W.R. Lethaby and Ernest Gimson. They were drawn to the box-edged borders, simple flowers and utilitarian planning of medieval and seventeenth-century gardens. The remnants of surviving historic gardens, the enduring customs and planting combinations of the cottage garden, and manuscript illuminations and illustrations were pieced together to suggest appropriate garden settings for new and old vernacular houses. These sources were an inspiration rather than the basis for a rigid formula. The artistry of creating an Arts and Crafts garden lay in the fusion of unflinching, utilitarian modernity with the evocation of a bygone age and its values.

OPPOSITE
**Robert Lorimer, Earlshall, rose terrace.**
© Martin Charles

BELOW
**Ernest Barnsley, Upper Dorvel House, Sapperton, 1901.**
© Martin Charles

ABOVE
**Philip Webb, Red House,
1859, showing 'The Pilgrim's
Rest'.**
© Martin Charles

OPPOSITE
**Philip Webb, Red House.**
National Trust Photographic
Library / Andrew Butler

PAGE 40
**Philip Webb, design for well
at Red House, 1859.**
V&A: E.64–1916

PAGE 41
**Philip Webb, Red House,
the well.**
© Martin Charles

In the design of Morris's home, Red House, Philip Webb envisaged the garden as a seamless extension of the plan and aesthetic of the new house. The same Gothic references and meticulous care for materials and construction that distinguish the building infuse every detail of the garden. A working well with a tile and timber conical roof is asymmetrically positioned within a rectangular lawn, framed on two sides by the wings of the house. It serves as a formal device, the focal point around which the house and garden revolve, but it also articulates a romantic naivity, a passion for medieval customs and traditions that was fundamental to the ethos of Red House and the subsequent development of Arts and Crafts.

The site for Red House was an old orchard on the ancient route of Chaucer's Canterbury pilgrims. Webb designed a porch overlooking the garden that Morris named 'The Pilgrim's Rest'. They retained the orchard rows of old fruit trees, devising the plan of the garden around their long, parallel lines.

Red House is regarded as the first Arts and Crafts house and garden because the house was designed as a creative unity. Webb began by shaping the plan of the house to suit Morris's lifestyle and domestic arrangements. The elevations were irregular as a consequence, and their character reflected the nature of the rooms they enclosed. Webb's elevation drawings are pencilled with

Scale 1" to the foot

very slightly wrot. and
if not too rough to be left with
the saw marks.

The whole of the work to be
put together in exact accordance
with the drawing, and the
specification to those supply
whenever practicable

over top of Post.

5 lbs lead plate

Iron bars of ironwork
½ square. wrot.

This is one of the plans
referred to in the agreement
agreed to give this 19 day
of Oct 1839 —

William Henly
Witness — Webb.

Elevation of iron gate. &c.

Plan of Rafters.

Tilting plate. a — 6×4

1" bolt

6×7

brickwork
all in mortar.

slate courses.

Half Elevation

Half Section

Cement.

| Letter | No | |
|--------|-----|---------|
| a | 1 | Ring p |
| b | 20 | Rafter |
| c | 20 | " |
| d | 1 | Ring co |
| e | 1 | Centre |
| f | 2 | Cross ti |
| g | 1 | upright |
| h | 4 | curved |
| i | 8 | do |
| k | 8 | upper ra |
| l | 1 | circular |
| m | 1 | " |
| n | 4 | foot p |
| o | 4 | " |
| | 1 | Bracket |
| | 1 | wind co |
| | 3 | opening |
| | 1 | Gate |

The Roo
pins to
require
the bru
the top
round

the names of climbing plants that were to clothe the walls of the house, and the first ideas for a garden, 'divided into many squares, hedged by sweetbriar or wild rose, each enclosure with its own particular show of flowers', are sketched into the margins.

Georgina Burne-Jones described the garden at the front of the house as 'four little square gardens making a big square together, each of the smaller squares having a wattle fence around it, with roses growing thickly'. Allusions to a medieval garden were extended in the more private courtyard garden on the south side of the house. A wooden trellis planted with roses originally closed the remaining two sides to the well courtyard, running along the side of the house to create a trellised corridor to the enclosure of square gardens at the front.

In the borders around the house Morris favoured simple, old-fashioned cottage garden flowers like roses, sunflowers, lilies and hollyhocks. Webb was characteristic of Arts and Crafts designers in his conviction that the formal areas of the garden should lie closest to the house, and that the planting should become more natural towards its boundaries, blending with the surrounding landscape.

A short distance from the house and its trellised enclosures the orchard rows of gnarled old trees were set within straight, parallel borders and edged with rosemary and lavender. Grass walks and gravel paths

OPPOSITE
**Philip Webb, Red House, seen from the orchard.**
© Martin Charles

ABOVE
**William Morris, wallpaper sample, 'Daisy, 2'.**
V&A: E.442–1919

OPPOSITE
M.H. Baillie Scott,
48 Storey's Way.
© Martin Charles

BELOW
M.H. Baillie Scott, Blackwell,
stained glass window, 1989.
Lakeland Arts Trust

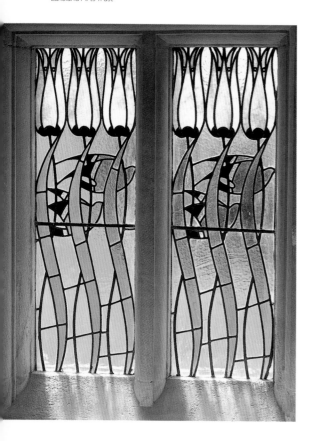

brought an element of formality to this 'orchard garden'. Its connections with the patterns and traditions of the surrounding landscape expressed a broader vision of a house and garden in harmony with nature. The order and simplicity of the garden requisitioned the fruit and flowers of Kent's historic orchards, and Morris's preference for flowers which could be traced back through centuries of English planting traditions was soon to take form in his decorative designs. The honeysuckle, daisies, roses and trellises that populated the Red House garden inspired his earliest wallpaper patterns, so that the ideal of living in harmony with nature spread from the garden into the house.

Arts and Crafts spans several generations. Red House was designed in 1859 but as late as 1930, when the poet and writer on architecture John Betjeman interviewed the elderly architect M.H. Baillie Scott, the same principles were still in full force. Baillie Scott began each working day by bringing a flower into the studio for his pupils to study. Carved foliage and berries, stained glass flowers and stylized embroideries and metalwork inspired by nature were designed as integral components within his interiors.

Betjeman recalled 'the presence of flowers everywhere' at his house, Ockhams, in Kent, 'in patterns, in vases and wherever you looked from the windows. Baillie Scott had designed the garden to provide small vistas from the house and when you were outside

in the garden the old house seemed to grow out of flowers and shrubs and there was, of course, a background of oaks and elms.' In his book *Houses and Gardens*, published in 1906, Baillie Scott popularized the poetry as well as the ground rules of Arts and Crafts garden making. He persuaded his readers to follow nature for economic as well as artistic purposes, and to develop 'the local characteristics of the land…A visit paid to a copse in the spring, carpeted with primroses and anemones, followed by blue-bells, and later with groups of foxgloves…. Demands absolutely no labour, and is a product of Nature unassisted by the art of man.' He argued that a garden was expensive to maintain 'chiefly in proportion to its artificiality and in the extent to which it includes mown lawns, bedded-out flowers and clipped hedges'.

He defined the basic functions of the garden as being 'to grow fruit and vegetables for the family and also to provide outdoor apartments for the use of the family in fine weather'. He recommended 'a union of use and beauty' in the smaller garden by adopting the cottage garden tradition of growing 'roses, lilies and perennial flowers, with a background of cabbages, potatoes and other vegetables'. Perennials were to be planted in drifts, 'bringing tall, bold clumps to the edge of the path' and, with the exception of dahlias, anything too tender to hold its ground through the winter was not to be tolerated. Creeping plants were encouraged between the 'masses of perennials', and flowers were allowed to 'shower their blossoms' over retaining walls with joints stuffed with wall plants. 'The same rough and homely treatment should be used in steps, and these and the walls should be considered as not being mere masonry, but building which is to be clothed with plant life.'

*Houses and Gardens* was illustrated with Baillie Scott's watercolour perspectives and garden plans to suit every size of plot, from the terraced house to the country estate. 'A garden of average size' included a lawn 'for tennis, croquet, or bowls…a rose garden, which may be square or nearly square in form' and a flower garden for perennials 'which may be long and narrow', together with an orchard and a kitchen garden, but the essential ingredients were reducible.

M.H. Baillie Scott, 'Heather
Cottage, view from north-east',
watercolour perspective from
*Houses and Gardens*, 1906.
NAL: 34.A.110

By abolishing the conventional lawn from suburban gardens ('it implies a certain cost of maintenance') a formal rose garden could adorn the smallest suburban house. A straight brick or stone path would create a vista from the house through the length of the garden, replacing the lawn to permit generous perennial borders to either side. In larger gardens a pattern of pathways, some contained within pergolas or enclosed by lime walks or tall yew hedges, connected the outdoor apartments.

The Arts and Crafts garden was 'full of mystery, surprises, and light and shade'. Even in the smallest garden, however, careful thought was to be given to the conclusion of a vista. Summer houses and arbours set within semi-circular recesses were favoured, and in smaller gardens a seat 'of good design and solid structure' sufficed to tempt the imaginations of Arts and Crafts homeowners into the garden whether the sun was shining or not.

The sundials, seats and structures strategically placed as 'centres of interest' in architect-designed gardens often echoed or exaggerated the visual themes explored within the house. In his designs for the garden at Norney, C.F.A. Voysey reflected the architectural theme of the building and its interiors in the form of a rectangular pond half enclosing a circular motif. Buttresses, bay windows and a covered veranda break up the building line and diminish the boundary

OPPOSITE
**Ernest Gimson, Rodmarton Manor, summer house.**
© Martin Charles

BELOW
**Edwin Lutyens and Gertrude Jekyll, Hestercombe, arbour, 1904–9.**
© Martin Charles

ABOVE
C.F.A. Voysey, Norney,
watercolour perspective and
plan, 1897.
Private collection

OPPOSITE
C.F.A. Voysey, Norney, pond
and summer house, 1897.
© Martin Charles

between the principal living rooms on the south side of the house and the terrace and garden beyond.

Voysey screened the servants' accommodation with a high hedge so that they could not overlook the family at leisure in the garden. He drew a long vista from the drawing room through the veranda, down stone steps from the terrace to the croquet lawn, and onwards towards the wilder, less formal gardens. The axis is accentuated by a sundial designed with Voysey's characteristic wit with four profile caricatures supporting a fifth caricature face in the dial's indicator.

In Britain the veranda was seldom more than an intermediary between the drawing room and the garden, encouraging a more flexible relationship between the house and its garden. In warmer climates, however, the veranda was promoted as a living or dining room 'for summer and for mild days in winter …it is like a summer house or an outdoor room always open to the sun and air'.

In *Craftsman Homes*, Gustav Stickley described the importance of light and the 'open-air life' to the planning of the modern American home. 'In all the Craftsman houses, as well as in the best modern dwellings of other styles, the veranda, whether open in summer or enclosed for a sun room in winter, is one of the prominent features.' Entrance porches were recessed or sheltered beneath oversailing roofs so that they could be furnished with willow chairs and settles 'and

ABOVE
**Gustav Stickley, front porch, from *Craftsman Homes*, p.101.**
NAL: 501.C.133

OPPOSITE
**C.F.A. Voysey, Norney, sundial.**
© Martin Charles

OPPOSITE
Charles and Henry Greene,
Gamble House, Pasadena,
sleeping porch, 1907–9.
Mark Fiennes

ABOVE
Charles and Henry Greene,
Theodore Irwin Jr. House,
Pasadena, 1906–7.
Mark Fiennes

PAGE 56
Edwin Lutyens and Gertrude
Jekyll, Hestercombe, pergola.
© Martin Charles

plenty of hammocks'. Sleeping porches opened Arts and Crafts bedrooms to the night air and the scents and sounds of the garden, and the most committed devotees of the great outdoors braved wind, rain and icy cold.

The contours and materials of the house spread into the pergolas, pathways and walls of the garden, and climbing plants were trained to soften and clothe the building's elevations. Leading architects and designers such as Webb, Baillie Scott, Stickley and Greene and Greene challenged Victorian boundaries and made 'the charm of living out of doors' desirable and accessible to the multitudes. Their traditional props: rustic building styles, the poetry of drawing materials from the land, the 'cottage' appeal and the spiritual and physical benefits of connecting with nature, made the Arts and Crafts style of gardening comfortably familiar and irresistible.

Arts and Crafts homeowners could afford to snooze in their hammocks or take tea on their terraces. The looser, more natural style of planting was intended to overflow onto pathways and scramble over pergolas and balconies. The fine art of managing a perfect balance between architecture and nature was a matter, according to Baillie Scott, of reacquiring a lost instinct for cultivating the soil but it was equally dependent upon a knack for relaxing and letting things take their natural course.

OPPOSITE
**Edwin Lutyens and Gertrude Jekyll, Munstead Wood, front entrance to porch.**
© Martin Charles

BELOW
**Gertrude Jekyll, Munstead Wood, iris and lupin border, hand-coloured photograph, c. 1912.**
*Country Life* Picture Library

# A SENSE OF PLACE

The Arts and Crafts garden was a secular Eden. It represented a retreat from the pressures of urban life and a return to innocence. However, many of the most famous gardens were also, paradoxically, public statements. Jekyll's idea of Munstead Wood as a secret garden within a woodland copse, and her insistence that the house should be approached on foot, with no convenient carriage entrance, is seemingly at odds with the garden's star status in her photographs and publications. Her hand-coloured photographs describe a perfectly balanced relationship between new 'Old Surrey' buildings (designed and built in collaboration with Lutyens) and her own ravishing brand of horticultural showmanship. They create an exquisite illusion of reality, substantiated by the apparent objectivity and relative modernity of photography as an art form. Open compositions with paths leading diagonally into the distance invite the viewer to occupy these intimate and secluded garden spaces, so that Munstead Wood and many of Jekyll's private commissions were occupied, in an imaginary sense, by thousands of visitors. Lifted out of context, the actual experience of finding them rooted in the Surrey landscape is replaced by an abstract understanding of Jekyll's profound commitment to a sense of place.

Similarly, Baillie Scott's watercolour perspectives occupy a separate reality from that of the houses and gardens they depict. It hardly matters whether his gardens were secluded behind the hedgerows of Surrey, commanded panoramic views across the Highlands of Scotland or never in fact took form at all beyond their paper reality. They were intended for publication and exhibition. Their presence as works of art and the ideals that they encompassed had a universal appeal. They were never limited to the particular conditions of a built commission.

The simple life promised by Arts and Crafts designers, and the security of a clear connection with the history and identity of a place, have an enduring appeal. Arts and Crafts houses focused attention upon the natural beauty of oak, cedar and stone, crafted in old country ways. In their gardens, swathes of bulbs and perennials that heralded the seasons simulated the patterns of wild flowers in their native conditions as if, by returning to nature, designers could reinvent a state of grace. This determination to encapsulate utopian dreams in the design of everyday objects and environments – to make the ideal real – can be seen as escapist or exemplary. It crystallized in the designs of houses and gardens as complete works of art around the turn of the century. These included houses such as The Orchard by Voysey; the Gamble House by Greene and Greene; and Gustav Stickley's Craftsman

ABOVE
M.H. Baillie Scott, 'Heather
Cottage, view from west',
watercolour perspective from
*Houses and Gardens*, 1906.
NAL: 34.A.110

OPPOSITE
Gertrude Jekyll and Edwin
Lutyens, Munstead Wood.
© Martin Charles

Farms, all of which were essentially private retreats yet at the same time internationally renowned.

The gardens at Hvittrask on the banks of Lake Vittrask in Finland were never famous in their own right. Nevertheless they exemplify the importance of garden design to the house as a total work of art. Like Red House a generation earlier, Hvittask was conceived in 1902 as an artists' retreat and a creative experiment. It was the combined home and offices of three architects, Eliel Saarinen, Armas Lindgren and Herman Gesellius, and their families.

The houses and gardens are half concealed within a spectacular rural setting. They are approached along a narrow track through a birch and pine woodland, which springs defiantly from a bedrock of granite. A stone gatehouse like a castle in a child's picture book emerges through the trees. It marks a boundary between the wilderness and the architectural oasis of the houses and their gardens. Beyond the gatehouse the dwellings and offices range around a central green.

Herman Gesellius and his sister Loja, a sculptor with a strong interest in photography, initially lived in the entrance building incorporating the gatehouse tower. Lindgren designed the north wing of the main building opposite for himself and his family, while Saarinen occupied the south wing. Both Lindgren and Saarinen were married and their two dwellings each had its own formal

Herman Gesellius, Armas
Lindgren, Eliel Saarinen,
Hvittrask, site plan, c.1907.
Museum of Finnish Architecture,
Helsinki

garden. The dwellings were linked by a
single storey studio where the three men
worked together.

Hvittrask embodied the architects' ideal
that there should be no distinctions
between art, life and work. The partnership
had already built its reputation through the
design of the Finnish pavilion for the Paris
World Fair of 1900, followed by the design of
the Finnish National Museum. The pavilion
was a statement of cultural and political
autonomy. It was designed as an assertion
of Finland's independence from Russia's
increasingly overbearing rule.

Gesellius, Lindgren and Saarinen's massive
stone structures and their idiosyncratic use
of towers, sculptural roof forms and robustly
carved details were an exaggerated reference
to Finland's historic building types and
native wildlife and materials. They brought
the architects international recognition as
contributors to an independent Finnish
identity. Hvittrask was a refinement of the
Finnish National Romantic style and a
statement of professional success. It was a
place to entertain potential clients, but it
was also a private exploration into the
relationship between art and nature and life.

Before the buildings were completed the
personal relationships between the three
partners had shifted. Eliel Saarinen fell in
love with Gesellius's sister Loja. The romantic
gatehouse tower where she was living as
their relationship developed became a

ABOVE
**Herman Gesellius, Armas Lindgren, Eliel Saarinen, Hvittrask, entrance building.**
Wendy Hitchmough

RIGHT
**Herman Gesellius, Armas Lindgren, Eliel Saarinen, Hvittrask, balcony detail.**
Richard Bryant/arcaid.co.uk

graphic symbol for their personal romance. It was carved into furniture and embossed into wall sconces in the house they later shared.

Fortunately, Saarinen's wife Mathilda also fell in love outside their marriage, with Herman Gesellius. A stained glass window in the Saarinen dining room portrays a woman in period dress seated in the formal garden at Hvittrask. The Saarinen quarters are clearly delineated behind her, while the panels on either side depict two attentive suitors. In reality, however, the relationship between the partners became strained. Lindgren left Hvittrask after only a year, and the partnership broke up in 1905.

Eliel and Loja Saarinen continued to live and work at Hvittrask with Mathilda and Herman Geselius until the latter's death in 1916. The artists with whom they had worked at the Finnish pavilion became regular visitors and contributors to the life and decoration of the house. The sculptor Emil Wikstrom made a granite bear for a grotto in the entrance court, a copy of the 'Flame' *ryijy* (a type of rug that goes across a seat and on the floor) designed by Akseli Gallen-Kallela dominated the main living area, and Jean Sibellius, whose music was performed in the 1900 pavilion, often played the piano for Saarinen and his guests.

Materials as well as motifs from the surrounding landscape were boldly expressed throughout the building and its interiors. The granite and timber of the lakeside

OPPOSITE
**Main living area, Hvittrask.**
Richard Bryant/arcaid.co.uk

BELOW
**Eliel Saarinen, Hvittrask**
**'Fairytale *ryijy* rug', 1914,**
**Indian ink and watercolour.**
Museum of Finnish Architecture, Helsinki

elevation, rising out of the woodland on a steep bank, are unmistakably drawn from the site. The tree-trunk pillars with log capitals that support the exposed ceiling structure above the open staircase in the great living hall speak clearly of Hvittrask's woodland setting. Built-in wooden benches were covered with *ryijys* depicting stylized trees designed by Saarinen and woven by the Friends of Finnish Handicraft. Containers and trellises were designed for the lakeside window in the living room and for the 'orchid room' adjoining the Saarinens' bedroom to house plants between the exterior and interior spaces. In the summer, according to one of Saarinen's graphic artists, the divisions between the house and garden were almost eliminated:

Summer in particular saw friends and relatives there, staying on for weeks or months at a time. The interior spaces were abandoned for the sunshine on the lakeshore or the tennis court or veranda and the agreeable shade of the arbour, where the pleasures of the dinner or coffee table were enjoyed.

Saarinen made watercolour perspectives of the interiors as well as the elevations of his houses and, in common with many Arts and Crafts designers, he had his houses photographed. The emphatic Finnish Romanticism and originality of Hvittrask earned it a place in such influential publications as *Dekorative Kunst* and Hermann Muthesius's *Landhaus und Garten* in 1907.

ELIEL SAARINEN A D 1902

It was represented in exhibitions in Helsinki and Leipzig, and helped to establish a clear identity not only for Saarinen and his colleagues, but also for Finland as an independent nation.

The political opportunism of constructing a cultural argument out of a house and garden and presenting it to an international audience was taken a step further in the German province of Darmstadt. Grand Duke Ernst Ludwig established the cultural supremacy of his region by inviting internationally renowned artists to Darmstadt, financing an artists' colony in an area of parkland to the east of the city called the Mathildenhohe.

Architects Joseph Maria Olbrich and Peter Behrens designed prototypes for a new style of dwelling, with artists' houses and gardens arranged around a formal garden and a communal building for workshops and exhibitions. Far from being utopian retreats, the artists' houses and their individual gardens were conceived as a public statement. They formed an integral part of the first Darmstadt exhibition of 1901. Roses wrought into iron gates and carved into front door panels welcomed visitors into the artists' inner sanctums. The ideal of *Gesamtkunstwerk* (that is, of the house as a total work of art), was demonstrated through elaborate interiors stamped with Darmstadt's distinctive stylistic hallmark. Nature was refined and abstracted to echo the geometric

OPPOSITE
**J.M. Olbrich, Haus Olbrich, Darmstadt, 1901.**
Photoarchiv Institut Mathildenhohe

BELOW
**J.M. Olbrich, entrance to larger Gluckert Haus, front door.**
Photoarchiv Institut Mathildenhohe

ABOVE
J.M. Olbrich, entrance to larger
Gluckert House, wrought
iron gate.
Photoarchiv Institut Mathildenhohe

RIGHT
Patriz Huber, catalogue cover,
'Gluckert House', 1901.
Photoarchiv Institut Mathildenhohe/
Patriz Huber

Patriz Huber, 'Sketch for the
daughter's room in the smaller
Gluckert House', 1901.
Photoarchiv Institut Mathildenhohe

formality of the artists' gardens through furniture, fabrics and wall and ceiling decorations.

A second exhibition on the Mathildenhohe in 1904 advanced Darmstadt's claim to a sophisticated cultural identity and cutting-edge style – a sense of place in the modern world. A garden restaurant, a concert pavilion and five circular temples designed by Olbrich introduced a festive extravagance to the parkland setting. Olbrich collaborated with the sculptors Ludwig Habich and Daniel Greiner to redefine the walled formal garden with monumental fountains, statuary and relief panels.

Whether historians label them as Arts and Crafts, National Romantic, Jugendstil or Art Nouveau, the gardens that were designed in Scandinavia and other parts of Europe at the turn of the century all regenerated vernacular traditions and local and national characteristics in order to combat the social and economic consequences of industrial growth. The arts, including the art of garden design, resounded with messages of political autonomy rooted in a long (and sometimes partly imagined) history of cultural distinction. In America, however, no single historic lineage united the nation. Progressive designers such as Frank Lloyd Wright and Charles and Henry Greene recognized the phenomenon that the key to the country's identity lay in its geographic and cultural diversity. The land of opportunity

OPPOSITE
J.M. Olbrich, Daniel Greiner, Luwig Habich, Wall Fountain, 1904, Mathildenhohe.
Photoarchiv Institut Mathildenhohe

BELOW
J.M. Olbrich, pavilions for the Second Exhibition of the Artists' Colony, 1904.
Photoarchiv Institut Mathildenhohe/ Joseph Maria Olbrich

was wide open to immigrant identities.

In their private houses and gardens, photographed and published for public consumption, Greene and Greene were keen to forge a connection between the house, its garden and the surrounding conditions of climate and landscape. They studied the architecture of California's Mission Fathers (early settlers in America), and in a 1905 article entitled 'California Home Making' urged their readers to lay the foundation for their houses and gardens 'in nature's own colour and form' by gathering together California's 'lichen-covered field stones'. They were never bound, however, by vernacular traditions. Charles Sumner Greene likened the modern Californian taste for living out of doors to that of the ancient Greeks, Romans and Japanese: 'In fact all art-loving people love nature first, then the rest must follow.' The desert sands of California, he argued, were equally hospitable to 'a Villa Lante or a Fukagawa garden'.

Houses such as the Tichenor House at Long Beach enclosed elaborately crafted Oriental gardens with stepping-stone paths, ornamental pools and Japanese bridges, while the U-shaped Culbertson house in Pasadena designed less than a decade later included a formal classical garden and an Italianate cascading water garden. Both houses answer Charles Greene's appeal for a 'house garden ... made to live in' with 'an arbour leading at the side to a secluded spot sheltered but not gloomy, where one may leave one's book or work and take it up again at will. Where one could look out into the bright sunlight on groups of flowers, and where one may hear the tinkle of water and see the birds drink.' They catered for an emotional sense of place set apart from the specifics of time and location, an autonomous world in which, even a century ago, the most precious commodity was time.

**Charles and Henry Greene, Tichenor House, Long Beach.**
Avery Library, Columbia University, New York

ABOVE
**Charles and Henry Greene,
Culbertson House, Pasadena,
1911–13.**
Mark Fiennes

OPPOSITE
**Charles and Henry Greene,
Culbertson House, Pasadena.**
Mark Fiennes

# LIVING IN A GARDEN

Arts and Crafts was essentially inclusive. It encouraged new societies and a sense of community. Town planning began to emerge as an independent discipline at the beginning of the twentieth century and Arts and Crafts architects were eager to shape the character of progressive suburban developments steeped in the ethos and aesthetics of the garden. Communities as distant as Oak Park in Chicago and Hampstead Garden Suburb in London were characterized by gently curving streets edged with broad ribbons of grass. Building lines were set back behind generous front gardens.

Architectural commissions and competitions engaged designers at the forefront of the Arts and Crafts movement, including Lutyens, Frank Lloyd Wright and Baillie Scott, in this great social experiment. They designed houses and gardens to be built on spec, or purchased off the peg as blueprints for self-build bungalows or modest suburban houses. Front gardens contributed to the general effect of artistic enclave, cottage rusticity or open simplicity, and garden clubs and societies supported amateur and expert residents alike. The concept of style as the exclusive domain of the wealthy was redundant.

The reforming effects of a generous garden setting and a modest but tastefully designed home, the ideal of living and working in harmony with nature, underpinned the garden city movement. In California, the poet Charles Keeler and the architect Bernard Maybeck both subscribed to the idea that

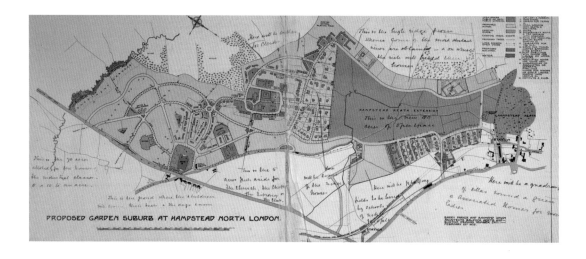

PROPOSED GARDEN SUBURB AT HAMPSTEAD NORTH LONDON.

OPPOSITE
**Barry Parker and Raymond Unwin, early plan for Hampstead Garden Suburb, 1906.**
London Metropolitan Archives

ABOVE
**Bernard Maybeck, Isaac Flagg garden, Berkeley, 1901.**
© Saxon Holt Photography

architecture and its environment could influence the morals and personalities of its inhabitants. Together they formed the Hillside Club, an improvement society in the Berkeley hills overlooking San Francisco Bay. According to Keeler the objective of the club was to persuade local residents 'to build their homes along certain approved artistic lines – low houses and broad lanais with plenty of yard room; trying to get people out of doors, getting them interested in flowers and gardens, and making the flowers and trees and gardens a more vital part of the home'.

The sloping contours and indigenous oaks of the northern Berkeley hills were incorporated into an immense woodland garden. Existing trees were supplemented with exotic species. Rocky outcrops were retained or worked into stone pathways and garden walls. Half hidden between the trees, Maybeck's rustic shingled houses commanded panoramic views across the bay, and their gardens blended with the woodland hillside setting. Maybeck's wife Annie co-wrote the aims of the club. 'We wanted to make sure that no hill street could ever be straight.' When business was good she bought land, but principles always took precedence over profit, even when times were hard. She only sold lots to 'nice young people who did not smoke or drink or get divorced'.

The Berkeley hills were populated largely by artists and intellectuals from the university nearby. They chose to socialize at the clubhouse designed by Maybeck, staging pageants and dressing up in his homemade medieval robes for the Christmas play. Their shared ideals and sense of community were self-perpetuating, attracting more like-minded residents to the area.

The character of Maybeck's timber cabins set within a cultivated woodland garden was uniquely suited to Berkeley and its alternative values in the first decades of the twentieth century, but Arts and Crafts offered a coherent identity, a distinctive style to neighbourhoods bound by material aspirations and notions of fashion, as well as to those compelled by moral and intellectual arguments to live the simple life.

Across America new residential areas were laid out and divided into lots, providing self-build opportunities for first-time buyers. Blueprint designs for craftsman-style homes could be purchased by mail order. They came with sheltering porches and verandas, and even if the garden features were not specified as part of the plan there was no shortage of books and magazines to guide new homeowners in the art of garden making.

**Bungalow Heaven, California.**
Wendy Hitchmough

OPPOSITE
C.F.A. Voysey, Broadleas, view
from window across lake.
© Martin Charles

BELOW
C.F.A. Voysey, Broadleas,
Windermere, service wing.
© Martin Charles

In areas such as Bungalow Heaven in Pasadena, California, well-tended gardens with climbing plants framing front porches and scrambling over elevations defined the character of the neighbourhood. The finely crafted details of gateways, paths and pergolas popularized in photographs of more elaborate architect-designed gardens were simplified for their fashionable appeal.

According to *The Craftsman*, the Arts and Crafts philosophy of traditional homespun values and honest craftsmanship was every bit as important to the design of modest bungalows as to substantial estates. Whether the simple life was bought in as a ready-made style, however, or adopted as a conviction, it had an improving effect on the material values as well as on the moral fibre of the district.

Areas of outstanding natural beauty such as Pasadena in the United States and Windermere in the British Lake District were colonized by Arts and Crafts clients and builders as rail networks expanded to meet the holiday market. Again, the garden settings for these new houses defined the distinctive character of their communities. In rural areas such as Windermere houses were often second homes. Garden walls and gateposts adopted the local dry stone walling tradition and the houses were set within generous gardens, half concealed in the landscape. The native trees and the glades of bluebells were barely disturbed by

the modest determination of Arts and Crafts
designers to work in harmony with nature.

The scale of the gardens, and the care with
which the natural lie of the land was preserved
in all but the most formal areas close to the
house, helped to safeguard and preserve the
natural beauty of the area. The views from
Blackwell, designed by Baillie Scott, and
from Voysey's Broadleas and Moorcrag, take
in Lake Windermere and the changing light
on the fells beyond. The rooftops and gables
of a few other houses appear through the
trees. There is a remote sense of community,
with like-minded homeowners gathered
around the lake, rather than a feeling of
isolation – but the overwhelming impression
is one of tranquillity, of a settled relationship
with nature.

The gardens to these country houses were
artistically laid out and planted, with terraces
leading from the drawing rooms or living
halls into the garden rooms beyond. Arts
and Crafts clients who took to gardening as
a hobby enjoyed a practical and profound
experience of engaging with nature, of
adjusting their pace to work with the seasons'
changes. The old-fashioned flowers and
perennial character of the Arts and Crafts
garden interpreted the movement's play on
tradition and continuity in a living form.
The balanced formality of its layout, the
dynamics of its vistas and the understated
craftsmanship of its garden structures
and pathways promoted a harmonious

relationship between the house, its garden and the landscape or neighbourhood beyond.

The simple life has a perpetual appeal. The Arts and Crafts ideal of living outdoors, of a fluid boundary between house and garden with spaces for eating and socializing designed into the garden, and images and materials drawn from the landscape forming the structure and decoration of the building, is still in force. Gardening has never been more popular as an amateur activity, a means of slowing down and connecting with nature's rhythms.

Armchair gardening, taking inspiration from lavishly illustrated books and magazines, has become ever more seductive and beguiling since Robinson's and Jekyll's pioneering publications and the introduction of the myth of natural planting as a style that takes care of itself, so poetically argued by Baillie Scott. Landscape architects design garden settings and open spaces into new communities, drawing on the local characteristics of the site and soil to identify a distinctive sense of place. Garden clubs and societies continue to bind communities together. The values and traditions that were revived and reinvented by the Arts and Crafts movement have been adapted to meet the changing demands of modern life. Nonetheless, the Arts and Crafts commitment to amateur involvement and to living and working in harmony with nature remains at the root of modern gardening.

OPPOSITE
C.F.A. Voysey, Moor Crag, garden and rear elevation.
© Martin Charles

BELOW
M.H. Baillie Scott, Blackwell, stained glass window.
Lakeland Arts Trust

# FURTHER READING

Baillie Scott, M. H., *Houses and Gardens*, George Newnes Ltd, 1906

Bosley, Edward, *Greene & Greene*, Phaidon Press, 2000

Brown, Jane, *Gardens of a Golden Afternoon*, Allen Lane, 1982

Darke, Rick, *In Harmony with Nature: Lessons from the Arts and Crafts Garden*, Michael Friedman, 2000

Davey, Peter, *Arts and Crafts Architecture*, Phaidon Press, 1995

Duchscherer, Paul, *Outside the Bungalow: America's Arts and Crafts Garden*, Penguin Putnam, 1999

Hausen, Marika, *Eliel Saarinen Projects 1896–1923*, Museum of Finnish Architecture, 1990

Hitchmough, Wendy, *Arts and Crafts Gardens*, Pavilion Books, 1997

Hamilton, Jill, Duchess of, Penny Hart and John Simmons, *The Gardens of William Morris*, Pavilion Books, 1998

Jekyll, Gertrude, *Home and Garden*, Longmans, Green & Co., 1900

Jekyll, Gertrude and Lawrence Weaver, *Arts and Crafts Gardens*, Garden Art Press, 1997

MacCarthy, Fiona, *William Morris, A Life for our Time*, Faber and Faber, 1994

McCarter, Robert, *Frank Lloyd Wright*, Phaidon Press, 1997

Robinson, William, *The Wild Garden*, John Murray, 1870

Robinson, William, *The English Flower Garden*, John Murray, 1883

Streatfield, David, *California Gardens: Creating a New Eden*, Abbeville Press, 1994

Tankard, Judith, *Gardens of the Arts and Crafts Movement: Reality and Imagination*, Abrams, 2004

Tankard, Judith, *Gertrude Jekyll at Munstead Wood*, Bramley Books, 1998

Ulmer, Renate, *Jugendstil in Darmstadt*, Eduard Roether Verlag, 1997

Weaver, Lawrence, *Small Country Houses of Today*, Country Life, 1910

Winter, Robert, *Toward a Simpler Way of Life*, University of California Press, 1997

**M.H. Baillie Scott, screen, 1896.**
V&A: T.127–1953

# GARDENS TO VISIT

Many of the gardens described in this book are open to the public, and the contact details for those in the UK are listed here.

**Blackwell**, Bowness-on-Windermere, Cumbria
M. H. Baillie Scott, 1897–1900
Lakeland Arts Trust
www.blackwell.org.uk
Tel. 01539 446139

**Castle Drogo**, Drewsteignton, nr Exeter
Sir Edwin Lutyens, 1910–30
National Trust
www.nationaltrust.org.uk
Tel. 01647 433306

**Dartington Hall Gardens**, Dartington,
Totnes, Devon
Beatrix Farrand, from 1933
Dartington Hall Trust
www.dartingtonarchive.org.uk/pages/dwegardens.html
Tel. 01803 862367

**Goddards**, Abinger Lane, Abinger Common,
Dorking
Sir Edwin Lutyens and Gertrude Jekyll,
1898–9
The Lutyens Trust
www.landmarktrust.org.uk
Tel. 01628 825920

**Gravetye Manor**, West Hoathley, East Sussex
William Robinson, from 1885
Country house hotel
www.gravetyemanor.co.uk
Tel. 01342 810567

**Great Dixter**, Northiam, East Sussex
Sir Edwin Lutyens and Nathanial Lloyd,
from 1910
Now owned by Christopher Lloyd
www.greatdixter.co.uk
Tel. 01797 252878

**Grey Walls**, Muirfield, Gullane, Scotland
Sir Edwin Lutyens, 1901
Country house hotel
www.hotel@greywalls.co.uk
Tel. 01620 842144

**Hestercombe Gardens**, Cheddon Fitzpaine,
Taunton, Somerset
Sir Edwin Lutyens and Gertrude Jekyll,
1904–9
Somerset County Council & Hestercombe
Gardens Project
www.hestercombegardens.com
Tel. 01823 413923

**Hidcote Manor**, Chipping Campden,
Gloucestershire
Lawrence Johnston, from 1907
National Trust
www.nationaltrust.org.uk/hidcote
Tel. 01386 438333

**Kellie Castle**, Pittenweem, Fife
Sir Robert Lorimer, from 1880
National Trust for Scotland
www.nts.org.uk
Tel. 01333 720271

**Kelmscott Manor**, Kelmscott, nr Lechlade,
Gloucestershire
William Morris's garden from 1871
Society of Antiquaries
www.kelmscottmanor.co.uk
Tel. 01367 252486

**Lindisfarne Castle**, Holy Island,
Berwick-upon-Tweed, Northumberland
Sir Edwin Lutyens and Gertrude Jekyll, 1911
National Trust
www.nationaltrust.org.uk
Tel. 01289 389244

**Munstead Wood**, nr Godalming, Surrey
Sir Edwin Lutyens and Gertrude Jekyll,
from 1883
Private ownership
Open days at end of April, end of May, and end
of June through the National Gardens Scheme
www.ngs.org.uk

**Red House**, Red House Lane,
Bexleyheath, Kent
William Morris and Philip Webb, 1859
National Trust
www.nationaltrust.org.uk
Tel. 01494 755588

**Rodmarton Manor**, Cirencester,
Gloucestershire
Ernest Barnsley, 1909–29
Mr and Mrs Simon Biddulph
www.rodmarton-manor.co.uk
Tel. 01285 841253

**Sissinghurst**, Cranbrook, Kent
Vita Sackville-West and Sir Harold Nicolson,
from 1930
National Trust
www.nationaltrust.org.uk/places/sissinghurst
Tel. 01580 710700

**Snowshill Manor**, Snowshill, nr Broadway,
Gloucestershire
Charles Wade, 1919–23
National Trust
www.nationaltrust.org.uk
Tel. 01386 852410

**Standen**, East Grinstead, West Sussex
Philip Webb, G. B. Simpson and Margaret
Beale, from 1891
National Trust
www.nationaltrust.org.uk/standen
Tel. 01342 323029

**The Hill House**, Upper Colquhoun Street,
Helensburgh, Scotland
C.R. Mackintosh and Margaret Macdonald
Mackintosh, 1902
National Trust for Scotland
www.nts.org.uk
Tel. 01436 673900

**Wightwick Manor**, Wightwick Bank,
Wolverhampton, West Midlands
Alfred Parsons and Thomas Mawson, c.1890
National Trust
www.nationaltrust.org.uk
Tel. 01902 761400

# INDEX

Page numbers in italic refer
to the illustration captions on
those pages

Alexander Morton and Co. *28*
amateur gardening 13, 84, 91
Amsterdam School 24
annuals 9
arbours 49, *49*
architecture 6–8, 16–17
  and gardens 58–60
  and national identity 22–3, 66
  as moral and spiritual
    influence 26, 84
  as politics 18, 20–2, 30, 66,
    73, *77*
Art Nouveau 76
artists' colonies 64, 73, 84
Arts and Crafts
  as fashion 20, 84
  as philosophy 20, 22
  as total environment 28
Ashbee, C.R. 22

Baillie Scott, M.H. 44–6, *44*, *47*,
  56, 60, *61*, 82, 88, 91, *91*, *92*
balconies 56, *67*
Barnsley, Ernest and Sidney
  36, *36*
Beardsley, Aubrey *19*
bedding 9, 46
Behrens, Peter 73
Bell, Robert Anning 24
Berkeley, California 84
Betjeman, John 44
Blackwell, Cumbria *44*, 88, *91*
Les Bois des Moutiers,
  Varengeville, Dieppe *23*,
  *24*, *26*
books and magazines 13, 18,
  22, 84, 91
borders 9, *49*
Bourneville, Birmingham 30
bowls 10, 46
Brentham Estate, Ealing, London
  *20*, 30
Broadleas, Windermere *86*, 88

building boom 20
bulbs 60
Bungalow Heaven, Pasadena,
  California 20, *30*, *85*, 86
bungalows 82, 86
Burne-Jones, Edward 16
Burne-Jones, Georgina 43

California *78*, 82
'California Home-making'
  (Greene and Greene) *78*
Chaucer 38
Chick House, Berkeley,
  California *6*
climbers 43, 56
cottage garden style 13, 18,
  36, 43, 46
*Country Life* magazine 18
Craftsman Farms, New Jersey
  60, *64*
*Craftsman Homes* (Stickley)
  53, *53*
*The Craftsman* magazine
  18, 22, 86
craftsman-style houses 84
craftsmanship 16–17, 32, 86, 88
Crane, Walter 22
croquet 32, 46, 53
Culbertson House, Pasadena
  *78*, *80*

dahlias 46
daisies 44
'Daisy 2' wallpaper *43*
Darmstadt 73–6
Darmstadt exhibition 1901 73
Darmstadt exhibition 1904
  76, *76*
Darwin, Charles 24
*Dekorative Kunst* 70
delphiniums 18
doors 6, *16*

Earle, Alice Morse 17
Earlshall *32*, 36
Elgood, George S. 9, *15*
elms 46

embroiderers 34
entrances *17*, 86
Ernst-Ludwig, Grand Duke of
  Darmstadt 73
Europe 76

Farrand, Beatrice 17
Finnish National Museum 66
Finnish National Romantic Style
  24, 66, 71
Finnish Pavilion, Paris World Fair
  66, 69
flower gardens 46
Folly Farm *6*, *13*
formal gardens 78
formality 44, 88
Fortingall, cottages *19*
48 Storey's Way 44
Friends of Finnish Handicrafts
  70
furniture designers 34

Gallen-Kallela, Akseli 69
Gamble House, Pasadena
  60, *55*
garden cities and suburbs
  20, 30
garden city movement 82
*The Garden* magazine 13, 14, 16
garden setting 82
gardens
  and architecture 6, 9, 14, 49
  as art form 9
  as hobby 10, 88
*Gesamtkunstwerk* 73
Gesellius, Herman 64–9, *64*, *67*
Gesellius, Loja 64, 66
Gimson, Ernest 36, *29*, *49*
Gluckert Haus, Darmstadt *73*,
  *74*, *75*
Gothic references 36, 38
Gravetye Manor, East Sussex
  *13*, *14*
Great Tangley *15*
Greene, Charles and Henry *55*,
  56, 60, 76, *78*, *78*, *80*
Greiner, Daniel 76, *76*

Habich, Ludwig 76, *76*
Hampstead Garden Suburb 82,
  *83*
harebells *62*
harmony with nature 10, 30, 44,
  82, 86, 91
Haus Olbrich, Darmstadt *73*
Heather Cottage *47*, *61*
Hestercombe, Taunton,
  Somerset *49*, *55*
Hidcote Manor, Chipping
  Camden, Gloucestershire *34*
Highlands of Scotland 60
Hillside Club 84
historical sources 34–6
hollyhocks 9, 43
*Home and Garden* (Jekyll) 16
Home Arts and Industries
  Association 22
*The Home* magazine 22
honeysuckle 44
*House Beautiful* magazine 18
*Houses and Gardens* (Baillie
  Scott) 46
Huber, Patriz 74, *75*
Hvittrask, Lake Vittrask,
  Helsinki, Finland 64–73, *64*,
  *66*, *67*, *69*, *70*
Hyde, Guy *6*

industrialism 22, 76
Isaac Flagg garden, Berkeley *83*
Italian renaissance gardens 34

Jekyll, Gertrude 9, *13*, 14, *15*,
  16–17, *49*, 55, 58, *58*, *61*, *62*, 91
Johnston, Lawrence 34
*Jugendstil* 76

Keeler, Charles 82–4
King, Francis 17
kitchen gardens 10, 46

Lake District, Britain 86
Lake Windermere 86, 88
*Landhaus und Garten*
  (Muthesius) 70

landscape setting  58, 64, 78, 84
lavender  9, 43
lawns  46, 49
Lethaby, W.R.  36
lilies  43, 46
Lindgren, Armas  64–9, 64, 66, 67
local materials and building styles  16, 32, 66, 69–70, 86, 91
Lorimer, Robert  32, 36
lupins  18
Lutyens, Edwin  6, 13, 16, 17, 23, 24, 26, 49, 55, 58, 58, 61, 82

Mackail, J.M.  22
MacLaren, James  19
Mallet, Guillaume  26
manuscript illuminations  36
Mathildenhohe, Darmstadt  73, 76, 76
Maybeck, Annie  84
Maybeck, Bernard  82–4, 6, 83
medieval gardens  36, 43
Meyer May House, Grand Rapids, Michigan  9
Michaelmas daisies  14
Mission Fathers  78
modernity  18, 36
Moor Crag, Cumbria  88, 88, 91
Morris, May  34
Morris, William  13, 16, 22, 36, 38, 38, 43
Munstead Wood, Surrey  13, 16–17, 16, 17, 58, 58, 61, 62
Muthesius, Herman  70

national identity  22–3, 66
National Romantic  76
native and wild plants  14, 60, 86
natural planting  13, 91
nature  56
   abstracted  73–6
   and art  28, 66
   and spiritual uplift  30
   as inspiration  13, 44, 46
   as primordial power  24–6

'The Nature of Gothic' (Ruskin)  22
Norney, Surrey  49, 50, 53

Oak Park, Chicago  82
oaks  46
Ockhams, Kent  44
Olbrich, Joseph Maria  73, 73, 74, 76
open air living  46, 53, 56, 78, 91
The Orchard, Chorleywood  26, 60, 62
orchards  38, 43, 43, 44, 46, 62
The Origin of Species (Darwin)  24
outdoor rooms  9, 32

Paris World Fair 1900  66
Parsons, Arthur  9
Pasadena, California  86
paths  6, 9, 13, 43, 49, 56, 58, 78, 86
paving  6
Pearson, Cavendish  30
perennials  9, 14, 46, 49, 60
pergolas  6, 9, 15, 55, 56, 86
philanthropy  30
phlox  32
photography  16, 58
'The Pilgrim's Rest'  38, 38
pinks  9
political messages  20, 66, 76
ponds and pools  49, 50, 78
porches  26, 53, 53, 84, 86
Powell, Alfred  29
Prairie Style  24
Pullman, Chicago  30

Red House, Bexleyheath, Kent  38–44, 38, 43, 64
Robie House, Chicago, Illinois  20
Robinson, William  13–14, 13, 14, 91
Rodmarton Manor, Cirencester, Gloucestershire  49
rose gardens  46, 49

rosemary  43
roses  9, 18, 32, 43, 44, 46
Rossetti, Dante Gabriel  16
Ruskin, John  13, 16, 22–3
rustic see vernacular
ryijy rugs  69, 69, 70

Saarinen, Eliel  64–73, 64, 67, 69, 70
Saarinen, Mathilda  69
Sackville-West, Vita  17
Scandinavia  76
seats  49
second homes  32, 86
sense of community  84, 88, 91
sense of place  32, 46, 58, 78, 91
Sibelius, Jean  69
simple life  34, 84, 86, 91
sleeping porches  55, 56
socialism  22
Society for the Protection of Ancient Buildings  36
Some English Gardens  15
stained glass windows  44, 69, 91
Stickley, Gustav  53, 53, 56, 60, 64
The Studio magazine  18, 19, 24
suburbs  20, 30, 49, 83
'Summer' (Anning Bell)  24
summer houses  32, 49, 49, 50
sundials  49, 53, 53
sunflowers  9, 43
Surrey  58, 60
Suur-Merijoki  70
sweetbriar  43
symbolism  26, 28

tennis  10, 32, 46
terraces  6, 32, 53, 88
textile designers  34
Theodore Irwin Jr. House, Pasadena  55
Theosophy  24–6
Tichenor House, Long Beach  78, 78
The Times  13

town gardens  10–13, 32
town planning  82
traditionalism  18, 32, 34, 76, 86, 88
trellis  43, 44
Turner, Thackeray  9

Unwin, Raymond  30, 83
Upper Dorvel House, Sapperton  36
urbanization  22

vegetables  46
verandahs  6, 49, 53, 84
vernacular tradition  36, 56, 76, 78
Victorian design and lifestyle  6, 9, 18
vistas  49, 53, 88
Voysey, C.F.A.  26, 26, 28, 49–53, 50, 53, 60, 62, 86, 88, 88, 91

wall fountain  76
walls  46, 56
water gardens  78
Webb, Philip  34, 36, 38, 38, 43, 56
well  38, 38
Westbrook  9
Wharton, Edith  17, 34
white gardens  32, 34
Wikstrom, Emil  69
The Wild Garden (Robinson)  13
wisteria  9
women and the garden  10
Wright, Frank Lloyd  9, 20, 24, 76, 82